Drat That Cat!

Gerald Rose

CAMBRIDGE UNIVERSITY PRESS

One day, Gran made a big blackberry pie.
"Look what I've made," she said to Dan and Vicky.
Curly the cat came to have a look too.

Gran didn't see Curly.
"Look out!" cried Vicky.
But it was too late. Gran fell over the cat!

SPLAT went the blackberry pie.
"What a mess," said Vicky.
There was blackberry juice everywhere.
"Drat that cat!" cried Gran.

"Never mind," said Dan. "Let's clear up."
They washed the walls. They washed the floor. But they couldn't get rid of the blackberry juice.

"Drat that cat!" cried Gran again. "It's all her fault."

But Curly didn't care. She just licked her paws, and she didn't like what she tasted.

"I know," said Vicky. "Let's *paint* over the stains."

Gran thought that was a good idea. She got some paints from the shed.

They painted and painted and painted.
Soon all the walls were a nice, bright blue.

"Lovely," said Dan and Vicky.

Curly came to have a look. She still had blackberry juice on her paws.

"Go away," said Vicky. "We're cross with you."

But Curly didn't care. She left blackberry pawprints all over the floor.

"Drat that cat!" cried Gran. "We'll have to paint the floor now."

"Shoo, Curly!" said Dan.
Curly jumped onto the sofa. She left blackberry pawprints all over that too.

"Catch that cat!" cried Gran.
Curly flew into the air. And then – SPLAT! She hit the wall and slid down.

"Poor Curly," cried Dan.

But Curly didn't care. She just licked her paws, and she didn't like what she tasted.

"Look," said Vicky. "Curly's left stripes on the wall. Let's add some more."

Gran tried to wash Curly's pawprints off the sofa. She washed and washed, but she couldn't get rid of the pawprints.

"Drat that cat!" said Gran.

Curly jumped onto a chair and then onto the table. She left pawprints wherever she went.

"SHOO!" yelled Gran, and Curly ran out of the room.

"We'll have to paint the table and chairs now," said Dan with a laugh.

"And the sofa!" cried Gran. "Whatever next!"

They painted the chairs, the table,
the sofa and then the floor.

Then Gran said, "Hurry up. Mum and Dad will be back soon. We'd better clean up."

They put the paint pots in the hall. Then they all went upstairs to have a wash.

Curly was licking her paws outside.
Suddenly she saw Bonzo – big, noisy Bonzo,
the dog that always chased her.

Curly was so scared that she ran back inside and . . . SPLAT! She kicked over a pot of red paint.

Gran, Dan and Vicky came downstairs. There were red pawprints everywhere. Over the table, the chairs, the floor *and* the sofa. Everywhere!

"Drat that cat!" cried Gran.

Just then, Mum and Dad came home.
"Oh no!" said Vicky.
"Help!" said Dan.
"I smell paint," said Dad.

"What's going on here?" asked Mum.

"We've painted the living-room," said Gran. "Do you like it?"

Mum and Dad stared and stared. Then they smiled. "Like it?" they cried. "We love it!"

"And do you know what I like best?" said Mum. "I like these pretty red patterns. They look just like flowers."

"Whose idea was that?" asked Dad.

"Curly's!" said Dan and Vicky, grinning.

"What a clever cat!" said Mum. "You can have cream and chicken for dinner."

Later, Curly sat by her bowl, licking her paws. This time, she liked what she tasted.